"I FILL THESE PAPERS WITH THE BREATHINGS OF MY HEART."

WILLIAM WORDSWORTH, 1770-1850
-PARAPHRASED.

"..I love you. Three simple little words, and yet never uttered or inscribed in ink by me to another living soul, only to you. I will never love another as I love you. I will never cherish another as I cherish you. I will always love only you..."

Renard, Duke of Roxton
to Antonia, Duchess of Roxton

With Love To

TABLE OF CONTENTS

OUR LOVE STORY

OUR LOVE STORY

The Letters

ATTRACTION

"Beauty made love to your eyes and gave birth to my unborn smile."
— CURTIS TYRONE JONES

THE REASONS I AM ATTRACTED TO YOU

Date

Date

Date

Date

Date

Date

Date

Date

Date

Date

GRATITUDE

"You are part of my story, memory and scenery. Thank you."
— Kim Taehyung

THE REASONS I AM GRATEFUL FOR YOU

Date

Date

Date

Date

Date

Date

Date

Date

Date

Date

FAITH

"You are a man with dreams. I offer my faith and support"
— SHANEIKA MARIE

THE REASONS I BELIEVE IN YOU

Date

Date

Date

Date

Date

Date

Date

Date

Date

Date

TRUST

"True trust is when we can't see or hear one another, but still choose to believe in our love."

— FALL IN LOVE, 2021.

THE REASONS I TRUST YOU!

Date

Date

Date

Date

Date

Date

Date

Date

Date

Date

Date

"THANK YOU
FOR COMING INTO MY
LIFE AND GIVING ME
JOY, THANK YOU FOR
LOVING ME AND
RECEIVING MY LOVE IN
RETURN. THANK YOU
FOR THE MEMORIES I
WILL CHERISH
FOREVER...."

— Nicholas Sparks, Message in a Bottle.

COMMITMENT

"There's a higher form of happiness in commitment......."
— CLAIRE FORLANI

THE REASONS I AM COMMITTED TO YOU

Date

Date

Date

Date

Date

Date

Date

Date

Date

FORGIVENESS

"Forgiveness dissolves the limiting beliefs placed on love."
— A'CHIENG ORETA

A SPACE FOR FORGIVENESS

Date

Date

Date

Date

Date

Date

Date

Date

Date

Date

KINDNESS

"Life has become easier and more beautiful because you saw the good in me."
— ROY T. BENNETT

THANK YOU FOR YOUR KINDNESS

Date

Date

Date

Date

Date

Date

Date

Date

Date

Date

FAITHFULNESS

"Before, I wanted to say: "I found love!" But now, I want to say: "I found a person. And he belongs to me and I belong to him."
— C. JOYBELL C.

THANK YOU FOR YOUR FAITHFULNESS.

Date

Date

Date

Date

Date

Date

Date

Date

Date

THE LOVE WE MAKE

"The soul yearns to make love. The ego wants to have sex."
— LEBO GRAND

WHEN WE MAKE LOVE........

Date

Date

Date

Date

Date

Date

Date

Date

Date

i love us.

TO REQUEST PERMISSIONS, CONTACT THE PUBLISHER AT
GIFTS@REASONSTWOLOVE.COM

FIRST HARDCOVER EDITION SEPTEMBER 2022.

EDITED BY ACHIENG ORETA
COVER ART BY ACHIENG ORETA
LAYOUT BY ACHIENG ORETA

PRINTED IN THE USA.

Lightning Source UK Ltd.
Milton Keynes UK
UKHW051125071222
413453UK00001B/15